S R A Specific Skill Series
for Language Arts

Grammar

Leveled Books in Nine Key Language Arts Skill Areas

S R A

Columbus, OH

The **McGraw·Hill** Companies

Cover: © PhotoDisc/Getty Images, Inc.

SRAonline.com

Mc Graw Hill | **SRA**

Copyright © 2005 by SRA/McGraw-Hill.

Send all inquiries to:
SRA/McGraw-Hill
8787 Orion Place
Columbus, OH 43240-4027

Printed in the United States of America.

ISBN 0-07-601710-9

3 4 5 6 7 8 9 RHR 15 14 13 12 11 10

GENERAL INFORMATION ON GRAMMAR

Grammar is the sound, structure, and meaning system of language. Traditional grammar study usually involves two areas: parts of speech and sentence structure or syntax. Parts of speech (nouns, verbs, adjectives, adverbs, pronouns, conjunctions) are typically considered to be the content of grammar. The parts of speech involve the *form* of English words. Sentence structure (subjects, predicates, objects, clauses, phrases) involves the *function* of the parts of speech.

The study of grammar is important for two reasons:

1. Educated people need to know and understand the structure of their language, which in large part defines their culture.
2. Knowledge of grammar gives teachers and students a common vocabulary for talking about language and makes discussions of writing tasks clearer and more efficient.

ABOUT *SPECIFIC SKILL SERIES FOR LANGUAGE ARTS*

Specific Skill Series for Language Arts is a companion to *Specific Skill Series,* a supplemental reading program that has been widely recognized for its effectiveness for over thirty years. The two series are designed and organized the same. *Specific Skill Series for Language Arts* consists of discrete units of practice exercises that target and reinforce fundamental language-arts skills. Units in both series are presented in multiple-choice format for standardized test practice.

ABOUT *GRAMMAR*

The scope and sequence for Books A through H of *Grammar* is based on traditional grammar study and focuses on parts of speech and sentence structure. The scope and sequence for each book is located on the last page of the book. Each unit includes

- **rule boxes** that explain grammar rules.
- **models** in each rule box to illustrate the language point being discussed.
- **multiple-choice exercises** for skills practice and reinforcement.

Four **Language Activity Pages** (LAPs) appear in each book. Each LAP is divided into the following four sections and reviews the skills practiced in the preceding units:

Exercising Your Skill reviews key terms and concepts.

Expanding Your Skill provides mixed practice.

Exploring Language shows how the skills apply to real-world contexts by featuring one of six forms of writing: descriptive, narrative, personal, persuasive, expository, and poetry.

Expressing Yourself includes two creative activities related to the skills. One activity is always a Work-with-a-Partner activity to encourage collaborative learning.

SERIES COMPONENTS

- **Student Editions:** Nine books in each level (A–H) focus on nine skill areas: *Grammar, Usage, Mechanics, Spelling, Vocabulary, Sentences, Paragraphs, Writing Process,* and *Research.*
- **Placement Test Books:** One book for each skill area includes diagnostic tests to place students in the correct level.
- **Teacher's Manual:** Primarily an answer key, the *Teacher's Manual* also includes reproducible student worksheets and further information on how to use the program, including classroom management tips.

HOW TO USE *SPECIFIC SKILL SERIES FOR LANGUAGE ARTS*

Placing Students in Levels: The scope and sequence, complexity of skills, and readability in Levels A through H correspond to Grades 1 through 8. Students may, however, be placed in <u>any level</u>. For example, in the second grade, a student who needs remedial work in a specific skill may be placed in Book A, an on-level student who would benefit from skills reinforcement may be placed in Book B, and an advanced student who is ready for enrichment may be placed in Book C or higher. *Placement Tests* help place students in the correct level.

Setting: This series can be used for independent study and one-on-one practice sessions, as well as in small-group and whole-class settings. It is also effective in after-school and summer-school programs.

Getting Started: Students must have notebook paper or copies of reproducible student worksheets (located in the *Teacher's Manual*) before they begin working. Remind students not to write in the books. Students may begin in any unit of any book, depending on the skill practice they need, although it is recommended that they begin with Unit 1. As they work through the units, students should record their answers on notebook paper or on the student worksheets.

Pacing: Students should be encouraged to work at their own pace, completing a few units every day or every other day.

Scoring: Teachers should score units as soon as they have been completed. Then a discussion can be held in which students justify their answer choices.

Internet Use: Some activities, especially those in *Research,* require students to use the Internet. Students' use of the Internet should be monitored closely for content appropriateness and safety.

Grammar refers to the basic parts of the English language and how to put them together to write sentences. Understanding grammar will help you communicate your ideas clearly and correctly when you speak and write.

In Book F *Grammar,* you will learn about
- Nouns
- Pronouns
- Verbs
- Adjectives
- Adverbs
- Prepositions
- Conjunctions
- Subjects and Predicates
- Direct and Indirect Objects
- Appositives
- Gerunds
- Clauses
- Types of Sentences

After you finish this book, you will be able to label words, phrases, and clauses in a sentence. Some of the words, phrases, and clauses in the sentence below are labeled.

INDEPENDENT CLAUSE   ADJECTIVE CLAUSE

Every ant colony has at least one queen, who is responsible for laying eggs.

SUBJECT   PREDICATE   DIRECT OBJECT   PREDICATE ADJECTIVE   PREPOSITIONAL PHRASE

You will also learn about different types of sentences. The sentence below is a complex sentence because it has one independent clause and at least one dependent clause. The simple subject and simple predicate of each clause is boldfaced. The subordinating conjunction is underlined.

INDEPENDENT CLAUSE   DEPENDENT CLAUSE

Worker **ants will defend** the nest <u>if</u> unwanted **visitors approach**.

By mastering the skills in this book, you will be able to use words correctly and effectively to communicate your ideas to other people.

Unit 1
Nouns

A **noun** is a word that names a person, a place, an animal, a thing, or an idea.
- A **common noun** names *any* person, place, animal, thing, or idea.
  woman   woods   rat   monument   love
- A **proper noun** names a *particular* person, place, animal, thing, or idea.
  Ms. Garcia   Blendon Woods   Rex the rat   Jefferson Memorial
- A **singular noun** names one. A **plural noun** names more than one. Most plural nouns end in *-s* or *-es,* but some are formed irregularly or are the same in the singular and plural forms.
  friend—friends   bus—buses   child—children
  penny—pennies   half—halves   series—series

The Everglades

Which underlined word in each sentence is used as a noun?

1. The <u>Florida Everglades</u> is a <u>wide</u>, <u>shallow</u> river <u>filled</u> with fertile marshes and
        (A)   **(B)**   **(C)**   **(D)**
high grass.

2. This <u>area</u> was <u>formed</u> thousands <u>of</u> years <u>ago</u>.
    (A)   **(B)**   **(C)**   **(D)**

3. It <u>begins</u> at <u>Lake Okeechobee</u> and <u>flows</u> south <u>toward</u> the Gulf of Mexico.
   (A)   **(B)**   **(C)**   **(D)**

4. The <u>4,500-square-mile</u> <u>ecosystem</u> is home to an <u>amazing</u> variety of plants,
          (A)   **(B)**   **(C)**
<u>including</u> cypress trees, orchids, and mangroves.
(D)

5. Huge <u>flocks</u> of birds nest <u>here</u> after <u>their</u> yearly migration from the North.
  (A)   **(B)**   **(C)**   **(D)**

6. <u>Many</u> people <u>enjoy</u> <u>bird-watching</u> <u>in</u> the Everglades.
  (A)   **(B)**   **(C)**   **(D)**

7. Fish, reptiles, and mammals <u>also</u> <u>populate</u> this <u>marshy</u> <u>environment</u>.
                    (A)   **(B)**   **(C)**   **(D)**

8. The <u>Corkscrew Swamp Sanctuary</u> in the Everglades <u>is</u> an <u>interesting</u> place to <u>visit</u>.
          (A)   **(B)**   **(C)**   **(D)**

The Flea Market

9. You can find all kinds of things at a flea market.
       (A) (B)   (C) (D)

10. Collectors look for bargains in old letters, coins, stamps, and postcards.
            (A)   (B)(C)   (D)

11. Some collectors specialize in old silver knives, forks, and spoons.
          (A)   (B)   (C)   (D)

12. Silver jewelry and antique watches are always popular and sell well.
     (A)   (B)   (C)   (D)

13. For those not into collecting, there are silk flowers and candles made of
          (A)   (B)   (C)   (D)
    sweet-smelling waxes.

14. Whole families come for the day and search for good buys on their favorite things.
      (A) (B)   (C)   (D)

15. There is a popular flea market held in Hartville, Ohio, every so often.
       (A)   (B)   (C)   (D)

16. Many bargain shoppers value fairness in a dealer's price.
         (A)   (B) (C) (D)

17. They look for items that cannot be found in most stores.
       (A)   (B)   (C)   (D)

18. Some people visit flea markets to find old toys and records.
     (A)   (B)   (C)   (D)

19. Others hunt for antiques, such as clocks, chairs, and tables.
      (A) (B) (C)   (D)

20. The next time you go to a flea market, remember that one person's junk is
       (A)   (B)   (C)
    another one's treasure.
         (D)

Unit 1
Nouns

A **compound noun** is a noun made of two or more words. There are three different kinds of compound nouns. Check the dictionary if you are not sure how to spell a compound noun.

- A **closed compound noun** is written as one word.
  - outdoors   bookmark   teammate
- An **open compound noun** is written as two words.
  - high school   dining room   sour cream
- The words in a **hyphenated compound noun** are connected by a hyphen.
  - sister-in-law   great-aunt   runner-up

Which underlined word or group of words in each sentence is a compound noun?

21. An old version of the modern wheelchair was invented by John Dawson in 1783.
     (A)   (B)   (C)   (D)

22. A showcase can display all kinds of goods, from valuable baseball cards to
     (A)   (B)   (C)
rare coins.
     (D)

23. You can think of your library card as a key to unlock your imagination.
          (A)   (B)   (C)   (D)

24. In a wedding party, the maid of honor is usually a close friend or
     (A)   (B)   (C)
relative of the bride.
          (D)

25. Nothing except for mail should ever be put into a mailbox.
     (A)   (B)   (C)   (D)

26. We said good-bye to our neighbors before leaving for vacation.
     (A)   (B)   (C)   (D)

27. Hundreds of planes arrive at and depart from the airport every day.
     (A)   (B)   (C)   (D)

28. If today is Monday, that would explain why I have this headache.
               (A)   (B)   (C)   (D)

29. Did you know that my brother-in-law is studying to be a computer engineer?
          (A)   (B)   (C)   (D)

30. The press secretary at the White House has a very important job, which is to
        (A)   **(B)**   **(C)**
hold conferences during which he or she talks to journalists.
                                                 (D)

31. There has been much advancement in technology during my lifetime.
          (A)   **(B)**   **(C)**   **(D)**

32. Have you ever wanted to take a ride in a hot-air balloon?
   (A)   **(B)**   **(C)**   **(D)**

33. My mother-in-law has worked all her life as a math teacher.
         (A)   **(B)**   **(C)**   **(D)**

34. Do not forget to take a notebook with you when you go to your next class.
   (A)   **(B)**   **(C)**   **(D)**

35. There is a wide variety of wildlife in the woods next to my parents' house,
          (A)   **(B)**   **(C)**
such as deer, rabbits, and squirrels.
            (D)

36. Up to at least one hundred inches of rain a year may fall in a typical rain forest.
      (A)   **(B)**   **(C)**   **(D)**

37. A solar eclipse happens when the moon passes in front of the sun.
      (A)   **(B)**   **(C)**   **(D)**

38. In schools today, many classrooms have computers with access to the Internet.
      (A)   **(B)**   **(C)**   **(D)**

39. The tarnished plant bug damages plants by sucking sap from buds and leaves.
        (A)   **(B)**   **(C)**   **(D)**

40. Having color-coded keys on a keychain can help people remember what key
        (A)   **(B)**   **(C)**   **(D)**
unlocks what door.

41. It is not uncommon for a rainbow to appear when the sun shines during a
(A)   **(B)**   **(C)**   **(D)**
light shower.

42. My cousin told me that our great-grandparents came from China to America
        (A)   **(B)**   **(C)**
many years ago.
     (D)

Unit 2
Possessive Nouns

A **possessive noun** shows ownership or possession of a thing, a quality, or a characteristic. Possessive nouns may be singular or plural.

- Add an apostrophe and an *s* (*'s*) to make a singular noun possessive.
    The cat**'s** paw print is on the table.

- Add only an apostrophe (*'*) to make most plural nouns possessive.
    The cars**'** bumpers need a fresh coat of paint.

- Add an apostrophe and an *s* to make most irregular plural nouns possessive.
    women**'s** voices   teeth**'s** enamel   mice**'s** tails

Clara Barton

Which noun correctly completes each sentence?

1. Clara _____ life began on December 25, 1821, in North Oxford, Massachusetts.
   (A) Bartons   (B) Barton's   (C) Bartons'

2. Her _____ goal was to give a broad and diverse education to its youngest member.
   (A) families'   (B) families   (C) family's

3. Clara grew up to be a teacher; several _____ had the benefit of her teaching.
   (A) community's   (B) communities'   (C) communities

4. Later during the Civil War, she gathered medicines and supplies and took them to Union soldiers; before long, she became the Union _____ choice to oversee all Union nurses.
   (A) armies   (B) army's   (C) armies'

5. After the war, Clara obtained President _____ permission to begin a letter-writing campaign to search for missing soldiers.
   (A) Lincolns'   (B) Lincolns   (C) Lincoln's

6. Perhaps her _____ greatest achievement was the founding of the American Red Cross.
   (A) life's   (B) lifes'   (C) lifes

7. The _____ mission today is the same as it was in the early nineteenth century, which is to provide help for people in need.
   (A) Red Crosses   (B) Red Crosses'   (C) Red Cross's

The Fourth of July

8. I awoke to the _____ light streaming through my bedroom window.

   (A) suns   **(B)** suns'   **(C)** sun's

9. Today was my _____ biggest and best festival of the year.

   (A) town's   **(B)** towns'   **(C)** towns

10. The day's _____ got started early with a 7:00 A.M. pancake and sausage breakfast.

   (A) activities'   **(B)** activity's   **(C)** activities

11. Then at 10:00 A.M. sharp, the floats and bands started forming at the end of Main Street by the _____ playground.

   (A) childrens'   **(B)** childrens   **(C)** children's

12. After the parade there was a picnic and lots of good food; then came the games, including the _____ favorite: a tug-of-war competition.

   (A) mens   **(B)** men's   **(C)** mens'

13. Later that night, the _____ glowing colors lit the sky; it was the perfect end to a great day.

   (A) fireworks   **(B)** firework's   **(C)** fireworks'

14. The Fourth of July is the date we celebrate our _____ independence from England.

   (A) country's   **(B)** countries   **(C)** countries'

15. Many people take their _____ during this holiday and travel to Washington, D.C., for the celebrations.

   (A) vacations'   **(B)** vacations   **(C)** vacation's

16. _____ and towns all over the nation have their own celebrations, such as parades, picnics, and fireworks.

   (A) Cities   **(B)** City's   **(C)** Cities'

17. The Statue of _____ torch represents the freedom we remember on this special day.

   (A) Liberties   **(B)** Liberties'   **(C)** Liberty's

18. This _____ history is an important part of our nation's past.

   (A) holidays   **(B)** holiday's   **(C)** holidays'

Unit 3
Subject and Object Pronouns

A **pronoun** is a word that can take the place of one or more nouns. A pronoun can be singular or plural.

- A **subject pronoun** is used as the subject of a sentence. It tells whom or what the sentence is about.

> **She** and Lola were winners of the contest that **we** sponsored.

Singular Subject Pronouns: I, you, he, she, it
Plural Subject Pronouns: we, you, they

- An **object pronoun** is used as a direct or an indirect object or as the object of a preposition in the predicate part of a sentence.

> Miss Ortega surprised **them**. (direct object)
> She gave **us** a trophy. (indirect object)
> My parents went with **me** to the ceremony. (object of the preposition)

Singular Object Pronouns: me, you, him, her, it
Plural Object Pronouns: us, you, them

A Partnership

Is the underlined word a subject pronoun or an object pronoun?

1. My sister and I have a small business in our neighborhood.
   (A) subject pronoun   **(B)** object pronoun

2. We mow lawns, walk dogs, and water plants for our neighbors.
   (A) subject pronoun   **(B)** object pronoun

3. My sister designed and printed a flyer on our computer; it described all the many services we offer.
   (A) subject pronoun   **(B)** object pronoun

4. Mother put them in all the neighbors' mailboxes for us.
   (A) subject pronoun   **(B)** object pronoun

5. It was not long before they started to call almost every evening.
   (A) subject pronoun   **(B)** object pronoun

6. Now there is plenty of work; our neighbors know they can depend on us.
   (A) subject pronoun   **(B)** object pronoun

Transportation

Choose the pronoun that completes each sentence.

7. Ming and _____ did our report on various modes of transportation.
   (A) I
   (B) me

8. _____ found many interesting facts about different kinds of vehicles.
   (A) Us
   (B) We

9. Did _____ know that Henry Ford did not invent the car?
   (A) them
   (B) you

10. _____ perfected the assembly line, which decreased the amount of time in which cars could be built.
    (A) Him
    (B) He

11. Orville and Wilbur Wright were early pioneers of the modern airplane; their experiments led _____ to much success.
    (A) them
    (B) they

12. Few people may recognize the name David Bushnell, but one of America's first submarines was designed by _____.
    (A) he
    (B) him

13. Igor Sikorsky's work in Russia around 1910 helped to give _____ the basic model upon which some of today's helicopters are based.
    (A) we
    (B) us

Choose the pronoun that completes each sentence.

14. Many people honor their loved ones on Valentine's Day by sending _____ candy and flowers.
(A) they
(B) them

15. Doug gave Tito and _____ a tour of Central Park in New York City.
(A) I
(B) me

16. Donna said _____ wanted to do something special for Memorial Day this year.
(A) she
(B) her

17. The 3-D movie in the museum was so realistic it seemed the picture was popping toward _____.
(A) we
(B) us

18. _____ and Geri sell cookies as part of the school's fund-raiser for the annual field trip.
(A) Him
(B) He

19. Vacationers sometimes avoid swimming in the ocean because _____ are afraid of sharks.
(A) they
(B) them

20. Our class wanted to help the environment, so _____ volunteered to recycle aluminum cans at our school.
(A) us
(B) we

21. My lab partner and _____ used a microscope to observe the ovules of different kinds of flowers.
(A) me
(B) I

Chicago

In which sentence are pronouns used correctly?

22. **(A)** My family and I are going to visit Chicago, Illinois.
    (B) None of we have ever been to the "Windy City" before.
    (C) Us don't have any relatives there.
    (D) Dad and Mom told my sister and I what to do to help get ready.

23. **(A)** The first thing us did was to get on the Internet and search for information about Chicago.
    (B) There were a lot of Web sites for she to look at.
    (C) We found a Web site that gave facts and statistics about the city.
    (D) The information there was a big help to my sister and I.

24. **(A)** Dad and Mom asked us what we had found on the Internet.
    (B) We told they about the baseball games we could go to.
    (C) Dad was excited; him and me are real baseball fans.
    (D) Mom and my sister like baseball too, but them are more interested in other things.

25. **(A)** Next Dad told us about the museums; him likes museums.
    (B) Mom said the Museum of Science and Industry had some exhibits that would interest she.
    (C) Right inside that museum my family and me could visit a coal mine or walk through an exhibit that was constructed like a human heart.
    (D) We were excited that we could also tour a real U-505 submarine that is located outside the museum.

26. **(A)** Another museum of interest to all of we was the Field Museum of Natural History.
    (B) We really got Mom's and Dad's attention when we told they about Sue, the world's largest, most complete, and best-preserved T-Rex.
    (C) She has a permanent home at the Field Museum of Natural History.
    (D) They both agreed that her would be something to see.

Unit 4
Possessive Pronouns

A **possessive pronoun** shows ownership and is *not* written with an apostrophe. Possessive pronouns can be singular or plural.

• A possessive pronoun can be used before a noun or by itself.

Jake's bike is new. ⟶ **His** bike is new.

Connie and Tim's project is the best. ⟶ **Their** project is the best.

My book is on the counter. ⟶ The book on the counter is **mine**.

Our car is black. ⟶ The black car is **ours**.

Possessive Pronouns Used Before Nouns	Possessive Pronouns Used Alone
Singular: my, your, her, his, its	Singular: mine, yours, hers, his, its
Plural: our, your, their	Plural: ours, yours, theirs

The Wildflower Safari

In which sentence are possessive pronouns used correctly?

1. **(A)** Mine Aunt Ruby called me bright and early last Saturday morning.
   (B) She told me we were going on a wildflower safari; I should be ready in an hour and bring my camera.
   (C) After driving into the hills outside ours town, she parked the car and got out a small book on wildflowers.
   (D) She told me to take a picture of every wildflower in hers book that we find.

2. **(A)** I told her, "It will be your job to identify the flowers."
   (B) Aunt Ruby pointed out the snapping dragon and it's interesting petals that look like a dragon's mouth.
   (C) The bird's-eye flower is a favorite of my.
   (D) Dried foxglove leaves and theirs seeds can be used in drugs to strengthen patients' hearts.

3. **(A)** The stem of a catchfly has sticky sap that captures small insects that try to steal its nectar.
   (B) I wanted to see a New England aster, a favorite flower of her.
   (C) Crimson clover needs much space of theirs own when grown with other flowers.
   (D) We learned a lot about different kinds of flowers after ours trip; we can't wait to go again!

Savannah

4. **(A)** Savannah, Georgia, one of mine favorite cities, was founded when James Oglethorpe established it on the bank of the Savannah River in 1733.
   (B) It was a dream of his to create a beautiful city right there in the middle of the Georgia wilderness.
   (C) Oglethorpe and Native American leader Tomochichi combined their efforts, and theirs dream became a reality.
   (D) Oglethorpe's plan was unique; it's series of city squares were really miniature parks.

5. **(A)** Houses, churches, and stores all had theirs places on each square.
   (B) Oglethorpe would be pleased to see that his' dream has survived such a long time.
   (C) Situated as it was on the Savannah River, the city soon became an important port where people could buy and sell theirs goods.
   (D) Cotton and tobacco became its biggest products.

6. **(A)** During the American Revolution, the British succeeded in their's plan to capture Savannah.
   (B) During the Civil War, Savannah almost lost it's unique city plan.
   (C) Union General William T. Sherman had burned his way across much of Georgia.
   (D) Savannah was somehow spared from the destruction caused by Sherman and his's troops.

7. **(A)** In the twentieth century, Savannah faced another threat to its' unique city plan.
   (B) Developers wanted the city to approve theirs plan to tear down many of the old structures and replace them with modern buildings.
   (C) A group of people established the Historic Savannah Foundation in 1955 to preserve and restore their historical buildings.
   (D) Today, if you visit Savannah, you will see buildings and parks so beautiful that you will not believe yours eyes.

8. **(A)** Mine favorite place to visit in Savannah is Forsyth Park.
   (B) Several movies have been filmed on its grounds.
   (C) Various groups hold theirs Civil War reenactments there.
   (D) It is a great place to take yours packed lunch and enjoy a picnic.

Unit 5
Pronouns

- An **interrogative pronoun** introduces an interrogative sentence, which asks a question. The pronouns *who, whose,* and *whom* refer to people.

     Who is the best swimmer?   **Whose** is it?   **Whom** did you ask?

     The pronouns *which* and *what* refer to animals, things, and ideas.

     Which is the best?   **What** stopped you?

- A **demonstrative pronoun** points out something specific. *This, that, these,* and *those* are demonstrative pronouns.

     That is the correct answer.   **These** are my brothers and sisters.

- A **reflexive pronoun** ends with *-self* or *-selves.* It directs the action of the verb back to the subject.

     Dante wrote **himself** a reminder about practice.

- An **intensive pronoun** ends with *-self* or *-selves.* It adds force or emphasis to a noun or pronoun already named.

     José and Eve **themselves** cleaned up the mess.

Kudzu

Which kind of pronoun is the underlined word in each sentence?

1. What is kudzu, you may ask?
    (A) interrogative   (B) demonstrative   (C) reflexive   (D) intensive

2. This is an easy question to answer if you live in the South.
    (A) interrogative   (B) demonstrative   (C) reflexive   (D) intensive

3. Gardeners thought they were doing themselves a favor by planting this vine in their gardens.
    (A) interrogative   (B) demonstrative   (C) reflexive   (D) intensive

4. Who told them about kudzu?
    (A) interrogative   (B) demonstrative   (C) reflexive   (D) intensive

5. When the Japanese brought the plant to this country, people liked it very much; that was the beginning of the problem.
    (A) interrogative   (B) demonstrative   (C) reflexive   (D) intensive

6. The vine itself is pretty, but the problem is it runs wild, growing over anything that doesn't move.
    (A) interrogative   (B) demonstrative   (C) reflexive   (D) intensive

7. These can grow as much as a foot per day during summer months.
    (A) interrogative   (B) demonstrative   (C) reflexive   (D) intensive

- Do *not* use a reflexive pronoun in place of a personal pronoun.

  Darcel told Carmen and **me** about the party. (not *Carmen and myself*)

- Do *not* use *hisself* or *theirselves* in place of *himself* and *themselves*.

  Luis finished the chores by **himself**. (not *hisself*)

  Jerome and Jarvis **themselves** locked up the building. (not *theirselves*)

- Demonstrative, reflexive, and intensive pronouns must agree in number and gender with their antecedents and verbs. An **antecedent** is the word a pronoun refers to.

  We went to the store by **ourselves**. (pronoun and antecedent are plural)

  The **mall itself** is beautifully decorated. (pronoun and antecedent are singular)

Is the underlined word used correctly in each sentence?

8. My dad and I decided to drive down to Florida by <u>ourselves</u> for vacation last summer.

   (A) Yes   **(B)** No, change to *ourself*

---

9. <u>Those</u> was a good idea because we needed a vacation; however, we did not expect to find what we saw.

   (A) Yes   **(B)** No, change to *That*

---

10. My uncle, who lives in Florida, warned Dad and <u>myself</u>, but we were still not prepared.

    (A) Yes   **(B)** No, change to *me*

---

11. It was a green vine that grew everywhere, even on the telephone wires; <u>it</u> were covered with it.

    (A) Yes   **(B)** No, change to *they*

---

12. It's amazing to me that vines can stretch <u>themselves</u> so far up the side of a building.

    (A) Yes   **(B)** No, change to *themself*

---

13. It's hard to believe that a few plants could spread <u>theirselves</u> all over the South.

    (A) Yes   **(B)** No, change to *themselves*

---

14. Dad <u>hisself</u> is really happy he doesn't have it in his garden.

    (A) Yes   **(B)** No, change to *himself*

---

15. My uncle told my dad and <u>myself</u> it's a good idea that nobody up north planted kudzu, or they would surely be regretting it now.

    (A) Yes   **(B)** No, change to *me*

An **indefinite pronoun** does *not* refer to a specific person, place, animal, or thing. Indefinite pronouns can be singular or plural.

> **Everything** in this room needs to be cleaned.
>
> **Someone** should be held responsible for it.

Singular Indefinite Pronouns	Plural Indefinite Pronouns
anybody, anyone, anything, each, either, everybody, everyone, everything, much, neither, nobody, no one, nothing, one, somebody, something	both, few, many, others, several

• Some indefinite pronouns, such as *all, any, most, none,* and *some,* may be singular or plural, depending on what follows them.

> **All** of the jackets are red.   **All** of the popcorn is gone.
>
> (plural)   (singular)

A **relative pronoun** is used to introduce an adjective clause. It connects the adjective clause to the main clause. Relative pronouns are *that, which, who, whom,* and *whose.*

> The movie **that** I saw today was really long.

A. A. Milne

Is the underlined word in each sentence an indefinite pronoun or a relative pronoun?

1. <u>Few</u> recognize the name A. A. Milne.
   (A) indefinite   (B) relative

2. <u>Many</u>, however, have heard of Winnie-the-Pooh, his most famous character.
   (A) indefinite   (B) relative

3. Alan Alexander Milne, <u>who</u> was born in England in 1882, had a happy childhood.
   (A) indefinite   (B) relative

4. Alan and his brother made up games <u>that</u> were creative and amusing.
   (A) indefinite   (B) relative

5. <u>Both</u> loved to write, and they were always making up riddles and stories.
   (A) indefinite   (B) relative

6. When Alan grew up, he got married and wrote the *Winnie-the-Pooh* stories for his young son, <u>whose</u> name was Christopher Robin Milne.
   (A) indefinite   (B) relative

Unit 6
Pronouns

- When the antecedent is a singular indefinite pronoun, use a singular personal pronoun to refer back to it.

  One of my sisters plays in **her** school band.

  Everyone turned in **his** or **her** report on time.

  Some of the water spilled out of **its** container.

- When the antecedent is a plural indefinite pronoun, use a plural personal pronoun to refer back to it.

  Both of the passengers had **their** tickets.

  Some of the girls have flowers in **their** hair.

Dogs and Cats

Is the underlined word used correctly in each sentence?

7. Everyone has <u>their</u> own opinion about dogs and cats.
   (A) Yes   **(B)** No, change to <u>his or her</u>

8. Both make good pets, but <u>they</u> are quite different types of animals.
   (A) Yes   **(B)** No, change to <u>it</u>

9. Both of my sisters have cats as <u>her</u> pets.
   (A) Yes   **(B)** No, change to <u>their</u>

10. All of my friends prefer dogs as <u>their</u> companions.
    (A) Yes   **(B)** No, change to <u>his</u>

11. Cats are independent; most can take care of <u>itself</u> very well.
    (A) Yes   **(B)** No, change to <u>themselves</u>

12. Dogs are more dependent, but many show <u>its</u> owners more affection than cats do.
    (A) Yes   **(B)** No, change to <u>their</u>

13. A cat is good for a person with a busy schedule because <u>it</u> won't need as much attention.
    (A) Yes   **(B)** No, change to <u>they</u>

14. Someone should never get a dog or a cat unless <u>they</u> can accept full responsibility for its well-being.
    (A) Yes   **(B)** No, change to <u>he or she</u>

A. Exercising Your Skill

You have been learning about different kinds of nouns and pronouns. Number your paper from 1 to 4, and answer the following questions about what you have learned.

1. Which is *not* one of the three kinds of compound nouns?
   (A) open
   (B) hyphenated
   (C) proper
   (D) closed

2. Which pronoun is *not* an object pronoun?
   (A) me
   (B) you
   (C) he
   (D) us

3. What two kinds of pronouns end with *–self* or *–selves*?
   (A) interrogative and reflexive
   (B) intensive and reflexive
   (C) demonstrative and intensive
   (D) reflexive and relative

4. Which kind of pronoun introduces an adjective clause?
   (A) subject
   (B) intensive
   (C) relative
   (D) demonstrative

B. Expanding Your Skill

Read the advertisement below. It gives details about a shoe sale. Number your paper from 1 to 18. Find the eighteen nouns in the ad, and write them on your paper.

Come in early for the best savings in town on all kinds of shoes. Every member of the family will find something for his or her specific needs. From hiking boots to ballet slippers, you'll find the very best quality in all our products. Our staff of experienced employees is ready to help you find just what you're looking for. Special hours for the sale will be in effect for Friday and Saturday.

C. Exploring Language

Personal Writing Read the journal entry below. Number your paper from 1 to 10. Then use the pronouns below to fill in the blanks. Remember to capitalize any pronoun that is the first word of a sentence. Use each pronoun just once. When you are finished, choose a term from the second box to label each pronoun you used. Some terms will be used more than once, and some will not be used at all.

we	our	everyone	himself	I	that	me	all	some	my

The Big Sale

_____ family and _____ went to a shoe sale on Saturday morning. _____ saw the advertisement for the sale in the newspaper. There were a lot of shoes. Right in the window of the store, I saw _____ _____ I liked. Both the style and the price pleased _____. _____ in the family found good buys too. _____ of us went home happy. Even Dad _____ said he had a good time. _____ trip to the shoe sale was a big success!

Types of Pronouns		
subject	interrogative	intensive
object	demonstrative	indefinite
possessive	reflexive	relative

D. Expressing Yourself

Choose one of these activities. When you are finished, give your paper to your teacher.

1. Imagine that you have a stack of paperback books that you want to sell. Write an advertisement that you could post at school or in a local supermarket. Write in complete sentences. Circle all the nouns, and identify each kind of pronoun you used. Try to use as many of the different kinds you have been learning about, such as possessive, interrogative, demonstrative, and so on.

2. **WORK with a PARTNER** With a partner, write a short script for a radio ad. Think of something you would like to sell. It may be a favorite book or a video game. The script should have a part for each of you to read. Perhaps you can think up some sound effects for your radio ad. Make sure you use different kinds of nouns and pronouns correctly.

Unit 7
Verbs

A **verb** is a word that shows action or expresses a state of being.

- An **action verb** shows what the subject of the sentence does or has.

  Juanita **sped** by me on her skates.

  She **has** new skates. *a.k.a.* ~~popular verbs~~

- A **linking verb** expresses a state of being or a condition and links the subject to a noun, a pronoun, or an adjective in the predicate. *Am, is, are, was, were, been, become,* and *seem* are some common linking verbs.

  I **am** nervous.   Ling **is** an athlete.   The sky **was** cloudy.

- A few words can function as either an action verb or a linking verb: *look, taste, smell, feel, sound, grow, stay, appear,* and *remain. become,*

  Luisa **grows** vegetables. (action verb)

  The audience **grew** tired of his speech. (linking verb)

Allen Say

Is the underlined word in each sentence an action verb or a linking verb?

1. Allen Say <u>is</u> an author and illustrator of children's books.
   (A) action verb   **(B)** linking verb

2. Allen lived in Japan with his parents until he <u>was</u> sixteen.
   (A) action verb   **(B)** linking verb

3. Then he <u>went</u> to the United States where he lived with his uncle and father.
   (A) action verb   **(B)** linking verb

4. In the beginning, Allen <u>created</u> children's books in his spare time.
   (A) action verb   **(B)** linking verb

5. At first he <u>trained</u> to become a sign painter, but this career did not interest him for very long.
   (A) action verb   **(B)** linking verb

6. I <u>am</u> glad he gave up that job because his books are great.
   (A) action verb   **(B)** linking verb

7. When his books began to win awards, he <u>became</u> a full-time author and illustrator.
   (A) action verb   **(B)** linking verb

8. Today many children <u>enjoy</u> his books.
   (A) action verb   **(B)** linking verb

a.k.a. Auxiliary verb

Verbs

A **helping verb** helps the main verb express action or make a statement. A main verb may have more than one helping verb. The most common helping verbs are forms of *be*, *have*, or *do*. Other helping verbs include *may*, *might*, *must*, *can*, *could*, *will*, *would*, *shall*, and *should*.

> We <u>**will**</u> **eat** dinner early tonight.

HELPING VERB   MAIN VERB

> We <u>**have been**</u> **eating** dinner early every night this week.

HELPING VERBS   MAIN VERB

- When a verb includes more than one word, it is called a **verb phrase.** The word *phrase* means "a group of words." A verb phrase is a group of words that acts as a verb.

> We **should have been finished** by now.

"America the Beautiful"

Choose the sentence that includes a helping verb. If both sentences include a helping verb, choose *Both.*

9. **(A)** "America the Beautiful" is an inspiring song with an interesting history.
   (B) The words of the song were written by Katharine Lee Bates, a young English professor.
   (C) Both

10. **(A)** In 1893, she boarded a train that passed by the golden plains of Kansas.
    (B) From the train's window, she could see wheat waving in the wind.
    (C) Both

11. **(A)** On that same journey, she saw the view from Pike's Peak as she was traveling through the Rocky Mountains in Colorado.
    (B) The sight inspired her to write a poem about the beauty she saw all around her.
    (C) Both

12. **(A)** Later, her poem was set to music written by organist Samuel Ward.
    (B) Through the years, different members of Congress have lobbied to make "America the Beautiful" the national anthem instead of "The Star Spangled Banner."
    (C) Both

Unit 8
Adjectives

An **adjective** describes a noun or a pronoun. It tells *what kind, how many,* or *which one.* An adjective can come before or after the word it describes.

> **That** basket contains **eight brown** eggs. The eggs are **fresh**.

- **Proper adjectives** are formed from proper nouns and always begin with a capital letter. Some proper adjectives are formed by adding an ending to the noun form. Others have the same form as the noun.

  > America—**American**   Japan—**Japanese**   Idaho—**Idaho**

- **Compound adjectives** are formed by joining two or more words together. These adjectives are usually hyphenated when they come before a noun. Hyphens should not be used, however, when the compound adjective describes a person's cultural heritage, as in *African American.*

  > **ruby-red** flowers   **steel-gray** hair   **African American** family

San Antonio

Which of the underlined words in each sentence is an adjective?

1. San Antonio, Texas, is the eighth largest city in the United States.

(A)   (B)   (C)   (D)

2. It is the only major Texan city founded before Texas won its independence

(A)   (B)   (C)

from Mexico.

(D)

3. Its German, Southern, Western, and Hispanic influences make San Antonio's

(A)   (B)

cultural life rich and complex.

(C)   (D)

4. San Antonio's Mexican American citizens make up sixty percent of the city's

(A)   (B)   (C)

total population.

(D)

5. The city's many festivals provide a diversity of good food: Mexican tacos and

(A)   (B)   (C)

tamales, Texan chili and barbecue, Southern hush puppies and glazed ham,

(D)

and German bratwurst.

6. In addition to country-western music, San Antonio is well known for its

(A)

German "oompah" bands and Tejano music, a unique blend of Mexican and

(B)   (C)

German sounds.

(D)

Unit 8
Adjectives

A **participle** can act as an adjective to modify a noun or a pronoun.
- A **present participle** is formed by adding *-ing* to a verb.

  The **cheering** crowd rushed onto the field. (present participle describing *crowd*)
- A **past participle** is formed by adding *-d* or *-ed* to a verb.

  The **exhausted** swimmer finally reached the shore. (past participle describing *swimmer*)

Sometimes an adjective can follow its subject. A **predicate adjective** follows a linking verb in a sentence and describes the subject.

  The river was **deep** and **wide**. (two predicate adjectives describing *river*)

Lexington, Kentucky

Which of the underlined words in each sentence is an adjective?

7. The city of Lexington was founded in 1775, seventeen years before Kentucky
   (A)   (B)   (C)
   became a state.
   (D)

8. It was one of the largest and most prosperous towns west of the Allegheny
   (A)   (B)   (C)   (D)
   Mountains by 1820.

9. Lexington has developed over the years into a very cultured place.
   (A)   (B)   (C)   (D)

10. There is, however, something else for which Lexington has become famous.
    (A)   (B)   (C)   (D)

11. Some of the fastest horses in the world have been born and bred on Lexington
    (A)   (B)   (C)   (D)
    horse farms.

12. Many farms with their fields of bluegrass have been the home of many racing
    (A)   (B)   (C)
    champions.
    (D)

13. Here is a postcard of an old, deserted barn that was once used for raising horses.
    (A)   (B)   (C)   (D)

14. Keeneland is a world-famous racetrack and national historic landmark in
    (A)   (B)   (C)
    Lexington.
    (D)

Unit 9
Adverbs

An **adverb** modifies, or describes, a verb, an adjective, or another adverb. An adverb tells *how, when, where,* or *to what degree.* Unlike adjectives, an adverb can appear in different places in a sentence.

> The door slammed **loudly**. *(how)*
> The grass was full of **extremely** small white flowers. *(to what degree)*
> We visit this park **often**. *(when)*
> I go **there** and sit by the lake. *(where)*
> I will be leaving **very** soon. *(to what degree)*

Holidays

Which of the underlined words in each sentence is an adverb?

1. Some holidays <u>here</u> in the United States are called <u>federal</u> <u>holidays</u>.
   <u>(A)</u>   (B)   (C)   (D)

2. On <u>these</u> days, schools, <u>post</u> offices, and banks are <u>always</u> <u>closed</u>.
        (A)   (B)   (C)   (D)

3. <u>Certain</u> businesses are <u>sometimes</u> <u>closed</u> on these <u>holidays</u>.
      (A)   (B)   (C)   (D)

4. President George Washington <u>suggested</u> a holiday <u>late</u> in November to give
      (A)   (B)   (C)
   thanks and <u>celebrate</u> the harvest.
            (D)

5. In 1937 President Franklin Roosevelt <u>proclaimed</u> that a <u>day</u> in October <u>should</u> be
                                (A)   (B)   (C)
   set <u>aside</u> for the observance of Christopher Columbus's arrival in the new world.
      (D)

6. We <u>traditionally</u> know <u>these</u> holidays as Thanksgiving, which is celebrated on
         (A)   (B)
   the <u>fourth</u> Thursday in November, and <u>Columbus</u> Day, which is celebrated on
        (C)   (D)
   the second Monday in October.

7. <u>Many</u> workers <u>everywhere</u> in the United States <u>appreciate</u> Labor Day on the
      (A)   (B)   (C)
   <u>first</u> day of September.
   (D)

8. We <u>dutifully</u> <u>honor</u> those who <u>have</u> served in <u>our</u> country's military each
        (A)   (B)   (C)   (D)
   November during Veterans Day.

Unit 9
Adverbs

- Adverbs often have *-ly* endings.
    easily   quickly   usually
- There are, however, a few *-ly* words that are usually adjectives. You can tell that they are adjectives because they describe nouns and pronouns. These words are *lonely, lively, friendly, lovely,* and *kindly*.
    The **lonely** man decided to make some friends. *(lonely is an adjective describing man)*
- Some adverbs do not end in *-ly*. They include *already, always, even, forever, late, near, never, ever, not, now, often, outside, sometimes, very,* and *well*.
    I **often** study after dinner.

Spiders

Which of the underlined words in each sentence is an adverb?

9. <u>Most</u> of the spiders in the United States are <u>completely</u> <u>harmless</u> to <u>humans</u>,
    (A)   (B)   (C)   (D)
    but there are two that are quite poisonous.

---

10. The <u>bite</u> of the <u>black</u> widow spider can be <u>extremely</u> <u>painful</u>.
       (A)   (B)   (C)   (D)

---

11. <u>Sometimes</u> a person <u>who</u> is <u>bitten</u> might have <u>trouble</u> breathing.
       (A)   (B)   (C)   (D)

---

12. The <u>person</u> <u>could</u> <u>even</u> <u>die</u>.
           (A)   (B)   (C)   (D)

---

13. The <u>bite</u> of the <u>brown</u> recluse spider can also <u>make</u> a person <u>really</u> sick.
       (A)   (B)   (C)   (D)

---

14. <u>Occasionally</u> <u>someone</u> <u>dies</u> from the <u>bite</u> of this spider.
        (A)   (B)   (C)   (D)

---

15. <u>Some</u> people <u>apparently</u> <u>like</u> to keep spiders as <u>pets</u>.
       (A)   (B)   (C)   (D)

---

16. My friend <u>once</u> had a tarantula that he <u>kept</u> in an <u>aquarium</u> on his bookshelf.
    (A)   (B)   (C)   (D)

29

Unit 10
Prepositions

A **preposition** relates a noun or a pronoun to another word in the sentence.
> The rabbit hopped **over** the log.

- A **prepositional phrase** is a group of words that begins with a preposition and ends with the **object of the preposition,** which is a noun or a pronoun.

> The rabbit finally reached its burrow **beneath the ground**.

          ↑   ↑

    PREPOSITION   OBJECT OF
                  THE PREPOSITION

- A preposition may have a compound object.
> Its burrow was near the **hedge** and the **leaf pile**.

Some common prepositions: *about, above, along, before, behind, between, down, during, except, for, from, inside, into, like, of, on, out, past, since, through, throughout, to, under, until, up, with, without*

California Facts

Which underlined group of words is a prepositional phrase?

1. The state flag of California, <u>which was designed</u> <u>by William Todd</u> and
                      (A)   **(B)**
<u>features a grizzly bear</u>, <u>will be one hundred years old</u> in 2011.
    (C)   **(D)**

2. A <u>threatened species</u>, the <u>grizzly bear</u> is also the state <u>mammal</u> <u>of California</u>.
      (A)   **(B)**   **(C)**   **(D)**

3. <u>More people</u> live in California than in any <u>other state</u> in the United States of
  (A)   **(B)**
America; in the year 2000, <u>the population</u> was just <u>under thirty-four million</u>.
              (C)   **(D)**

4. California is known <u>for its agriculture</u>, but <u>many people</u> also <u>recognize it</u> as a
                (A)   **(B)**   **(C)**
leader in the <u>entertainment industry</u>.
        (D)

5. The Colorado River winds <u>along the southeast border</u> of California and
      (A)   **(B)**
<u>forms the border</u> between <u>California and Arizona</u>.
    (C)   **(D)**

6. Although California covers 163,707 square miles, it is
      (A)
actually the third largest state in the United States, following Alaska and Texas.
     (B)   **(C)**   **(D)**

Bugs

7. Not all insects are bugs; bugs form a distinct group of over
       (A)   **(B)**
   eighty thousand species within the insect world.
         (C)   **(D)**

8. There are various types of bugs, ranging from familiar garden aphids to pests
       (A)   **(B)**   **(C)**
   that destroy crops.
       (D)

9. Some bugs are tiny herbivores, but others are carnivores that are
         (A)   **(B)**
   nearly the size of a human hand.
     (C)   **(D)**

10. While some bugs are covered with brilliant, metallic colors, others are
        (A)   **(B)**   **(C)**
    effectively camouflaged.
        (D)

11. Some blood-feeding bugs carry diseases that can be fatal for human beings.
        (A)   **(B)**   **(C)**   **(D)**

12. Stink bugs have pores that release a bad-smelling substance
          (A)   **(B)**
    that often keeps them from getting eaten by birds.
        (C)   **(D)**

13. Giant water bugs, eaten as a treat by people in some parts of China,
      (A)   **(B)**
    can swim and fly very well.
      (C)   **(D)**

14. A tree bark bug blends in so well with its environment, you
        (A)   **(B)**
    can hardly tell the bug from the bark.
        (C)   **(D)**

15. Red bugs feed on the juices of rotting vegetation and, not surprisingly,
      (A)   **(B)**   **(C)**
    have a bright red color.
        (D)

A **conjunction** connects words, phrases, or clauses in a sentence.

- A **coordinating conjunction** connects compound parts of a sentence. *And, but, or, so, for, yet,* and *nor* are coordinating conjunctions.

    Claudia **and** Rena are good athletes. (*and* connects two nouns)

    Claudia is a sprinter, **but** Rena is a long-distance runner. (*but* connects two independent clauses)

- A **subordinating conjunction** introduces a dependent, or subordinate, clause. Remember that a dependent clause is *not* a sentence and cannot stand alone. Even though it has a subject and a verb, it does *not* express a complete thought. *After, although, as, because, before, if, since, than, though, unless, until, when, whenever, where, wherever,* and *while* are common subordinating conjunctions.

    Li finished her homework **while** I waited.

    ↑

    SUBORDINATE CLAUSE

Beetles

What type of conjunction is the underlined word?

1. <u>Although</u> they are both insects, beetles and bugs are not the same.
   (A) coordinating conjunction **(B)** subordinating conjunction

2. A beetle's body is divided into three parts: the head, the thorax, <u>and</u> the abdomen.
   (A) coordinating conjunction **(B)** subordinating conjunction

3. All beetles have antennae <u>and</u> biting mouthparts.
   (A) coordinating conjunction **(B)** subordinating conjunction

4. Some beetles are less than one-hundredth of an inch in size <u>while</u> others measure six inches.
   (A) coordinating conjunction **(B)** subordinating conjunction

5. Some beetles are valuable members of their ecosystem, <u>but</u> others are considered pests.
   (A) coordinating conjunction **(B)** subordinating conjunction

6. The vast majority of beetles can fly, <u>though</u> there are a few types that are completely flightless.
   (A) coordinating conjunction **(B)** subordinating conjunction

Unit 11
Conjunctions

Correlative conjunctions, such as *either/or, neither/nor,* and *both/and* work in pairs to connect compound parts of a sentence.

> **Both** Wesley **and** Tyrell are on the basketball team.

- Notice that when you join a compound subject with *or* or *nor,* the verb should agree with the subject that is closest to it.

> **Neither** the boys **nor** their coach <u>is</u> in the gym right now. (singular verb *is* agrees with *coach*)
>
> **Neither** the manager **nor** the other players <u>know</u> where they are. (plural verb *know* agrees with *players*)

Pests

What type of conjunction is underlined in each sentence?

7. Pests are defined as plants or animals that are harmful to people <u>or</u> crops.
   (A) coordinating   **(B)** subordinating   **(C)** correlative

---

8. Some pests cause diseases in people, <u>but</u> others cause problems for the environment.
   (A) coordinating   **(B)** subordinating   **(C)** correlative

---

9. Pests are good at <u>both</u> finding <u>and</u> getting established in new habitats.
   (A) coordinating   **(B)** subordinating   **(C)** correlative

---

10. <u>Although</u> pests do very well on their own, people make it easier for them to spread.
   (A) coordinating   **(B)** subordinating   **(C)** correlative

---

11. <u>When</u> people interfere with the balance of nature, pests spread and multiply.
   (A) coordinating   **(B)** subordinating   **(C)** correlative

---

12. The quality of human life is affected <u>whenever</u> the pest population gets too high.
   (A) coordinating   **(B)** subordinating   **(C)** correlative

---

13. <u>Neither</u> termites <u>nor</u> cockroaches are welcome guests in any home.
   (A) coordinating   **(B)** subordinating   **(C)** correlative

---

14. If you get one or more of these kinds of pests, <u>either</u> call an exterminator <u>or</u> find another way to get rid of them.
   (A) coordinating   **(B)** subordinating   **(C)** correlative

A. Exercising Your Skill

You have been learning about verbs, adjectives, adverbs, prepositions, and conjunctions. Number your paper from 1 to 3, and answer the following questions about what you have learned.

1. What is the difference between a linking verb and a helping verb?
   (A) A linking verb links two sentences together; a helping verb helps make the meaning of a sentence clearer.
   (B) A linking verb expresses a state of being and links the subject to a noun, a pronoun, or an adjective in the predicate; a helping verb helps the main verb express an action or make a statement.
   (C) A linking verb can also be an action verb; a helping verb is never used to express action.

2. When does a compound adjective usually need hyphens?
   (A) when it follows the noun it modifies
   (B) when the adjectives are really long
   (C) when it comes before the noun it modifies

3. How does the adverb function in this sentence, and what word does it modify?
   We were too late to see the early movie.
   (A) tells *to what degree* and modifies the adjective *late*
   (B) tells *where* and modifies the noun *we*
   (C) tells *when* and modifies the adjective *early*

B. Expanding Your Skill

Number your paper from 1 to 5. Identify the underlined word in each sentence below.

1. The slug moves slowly over a rock.
   (A) noun   (B) adverb   (C) adjective   (D) preposition

2. Snakes and lizards are cold-blooded animals.
   (A) verb   (B) preposition   (C) conjunction   (D) noun

3. A hawk can spot a mouse from a far distance.
   (A) preposition   (B) adverb   (C) adjective   (D) conjunction

4. An injured zebra is prey for a hungry lion.
   (A) adverb   (B) preposition   (C) verb   (D) adjective

5. The nimble squirrel jumps from limb to limb.
   (A) verb   (B) noun   (C) adverb   (D) preposition

C. Exploring Language

Expository Writing Read the news story below. Number your paper from 1 to 10. Identify the underlined word or group of words by writing **P** for preposition, **PP** for prepositional phrase, **CC** for coordinating conjunction, or **SC** for subordinating conjunction.

Recycling Campaign Very Successful

The recycling center's recent advertising campaign has paid off **(1)** in a big way. Cars **(2)** and trucks arrived all weekend **(3)** with loads **(4)** of paper, plastic, metal, and glass. **(5)** When the materials are sorted, they will be sent to Sunnydale **(6)** or Riverton for processing. **(7)** After the center closed **(8)** for the day, Mr. Gomez, the center's manager, expressed his satisfaction with the community's response. He thinks this campaign could turn into an annual event **(9)** if the town gets **(10)** behind it.

D. Expressing Yourself

Choose one of these activities. When you are finished, give your paper to your teacher.

1. **WORK with a PARTNER** With a partner, write a news story about something happening in your school, such as a science fair or a spelling bee. Remember that a good news story answers the questions *who, what, when, where,* and *why.* Use some adjectives and adverbs in your news story. Prepositional phrases can also add interesting details. Keep track of how many of each you use. Remember to write in complete sentences. How many adjectives, adverbs, and prepositional phrases did you use?

2. Imagine that you are a photographer for a local newspaper. Find an interesting picture from a newspaper or a magazine, and write a caption for it. Remember, a caption describes the picture and tells what is happening in it. You should use colorful verbs and adjectives in your caption. Try to write all the verbs in the active voice. Share your picture and caption with the class.

Unit 12
Subjects and Predicates

A **sentence** has two main parts: a **subject** and a **predicate.**
- The **subject** part of a sentence tells what or whom the sentence is about.
    The **dog** belongs to Laura.
- The **simple subject** is the main word or word group in the subject.
    His **name** is Rover.
- The **complete subject** includes the simple subject plus all the words that describe it.
    That small gray dog belongs to Laura.

Rays

Which underlined word in each sentence is the simple subject?

1. A <u>ray</u> <u>is</u> a <u>type</u> of <u>fish</u> with a skeleton not made of bone.
     (A)(B) (C)   (D)

2. Its <u>skeleton</u> is <u>made</u> of a strong, flexible <u>material</u> called *cartilage.*
     (A)   (B)   (C)   (D)

3. The <u>thin</u>, <u>flat</u> <u>body</u> of a <u>ray</u> is well suited for its life on the bottom of the sea.
     (A) (B) (C)   (D)

4. The <u>ray's</u> <u>mouth</u> with its <u>powerful</u> <u>jaws</u> is on the underside of its body.
      (A)   (B)   (C)   (D)

5. Its <u>strong</u> <u>teeth</u> with their flat, broad surfaces can <u>crush</u> the <u>shells</u> of prey.
      (A)   (B)   (C)   (D)

6. <u>Their</u> <u>large</u> <u>wing-like</u> <u>fins</u> flap to move them through the water.
     (A) (B)   (C)   (D)

7. A <u>manta ray</u> is the largest <u>kind</u> of <u>ray</u> and is related to <u>sharks</u>.
       (A)   (B)   (C)   (D)

8. While <u>many</u> rays are able to <u>sting</u>, a <u>manta ray</u> is <u>harmless</u>.
       (A)   (B)   (C)   (D)

9. <u>These</u> <u>acrobatic</u> <u>animals</u> can even jump out of <u>water</u>.
     (A)   (B)   (C)   (D)

10. <u>You</u> may see <u>one</u> of these interesting <u>creatures</u> at an animal water <u>park</u>.
      (A)   (B)   (C)   (D)

- A **compound subject** is made of two or more simple subjects that have the same predicate. Compound subjects are joined by the conjunctions *and, or, both/and, either/or,* or *neither/nor.*

  Both **Laura** and her **sister** take care of the dog. (two subjects connected by a correlative conjunction)

The Anglerfish

Does the underlined complete subject contain only one simple subject, or does it contain a compound subject?

11. Deep-sea inhabitants such as the anglerfish are strange-looking creatures.
   (A) simple subject
   (B) compound subject

12. These oddly shaped and strangely colored fish lurk at the bottom of the ocean.
   (A) simple subject
   (B) compound subject

13. Fish and shrimp are a main source of food for the angler.
   (A) simple subject
   (B) compound subject

14. A large stretchy stomach allows the anglerfish to consume huge meals.
   (A) simple subject
   (B) compound subject

15. Neither you nor I will probably ever see a live anglerfish.
   (A) simple subject
   (B) compound subject

16. This fish's jaws can open very wide to take in prey.
   (A) simple subject
   (B) compound subject

17. Glowing bacteria in a lure on the head of the anglerfish attract prey.
   (A) simple subject
   (B) compound subject

18. Among anglerfish, the male and the female have many differences; for one, only the female has a glowing lure.
   (A) simple subject
   (B) compound subject

Unit 12
Subjects and Predicates

- The **predicate** part of a sentence tells what the subject does, has, is, or is like.
    The dog **has a lot of energy**.
- The **simple predicate** (verb) is the main word or word group in the predicate.
    He **chases** anything that moves.
- The **complete predicate** includes the simple predicate plus all the words that describe it.
    The dog <u>raced</u> **excitedly after the stick**.

Hungry Bacteria

Which underlined word in each sentence is the simple predicate?

19. People cause many problems for the environment.
    (A)   (B)   (C)   (D)

20. Huge tankers spill oil in oceans and on beaches.
    (A)   (B)   (C)(D)

21. Sometimes manufactured goods produce poisonous by-products.
    (A)   (B)   (C)   (D)

22. These substances are dangerous to most living things.
    (A)   (B)   (C)   (D)

23. Certain types of bacteria change poisonous chemicals into harmless
    (A)   (B)   (C)   (D)
    substances.

24. These bacteria use the poisonous substances for food.
    (A)   (B)   (C)   (D)

25. Bacteria grow in a wide variety of habitats and conditions.
    (A)   (B)   (C)   (D)

26. Even though some kinds may be harmful, bacteria plays important roles in the
    (A)   (B)   (C)   (D)
    world's ecosystem.

Unit 12
Subjects and Predicates

- A **compound predicate** is made of two or more simple predicates (verbs) that have the same subject and are joined by a conjunction.

  The children **splashed** and **played** in the water. (two simple predicates connected by a coordinating conjunction)

Molds

Does the underlined complete predicate contain only one simple predicate, or does it contain a compound predicate?

27. Spoiled food <u>often contains strange-looking living things</u>.
    - (A) simple predicate
    - (B) compound predicate

28. These living things <u>are molds</u>.
    - (A) simple predicate
    - (B) compound predicate

29. Molds <u>are made of many cells and can sometimes be seen with the naked eye</u>.
    - (A) simple predicate
    - (B) compound predicate

30. A mold <u>gets its food from spoiled food</u>.
    - (A) simple predicate
    - (B) compound predicate

31. The mold <u>breaks the spoiled food down into simpler substances</u>.
    - (A) simple predicate
    - (B) compound predicate

32. Molds <u>change spoiled food into something helpful to human beings or make something that is harmful</u>.
    - (A) simple predicate
    - (B) compound predicate

33. One kind of helpful mold <u>is a source of the medicine called *penicillin*</u>.
    - (A) simple predicate
    - (B) compound predicate

34. Many people <u>cough and sneeze around mold</u>.
    - (A) simple predicate
    - (B) compound predicate

Unit 13
Direct and Indirect Objects

A **direct object** is a noun or a pronoun that receives the action of a verb. It answers the question *what* or *whom* and always comes after an action verb. A sentence may have a compound direct object.

> Laveda brought **peaches** to the picnic. (direct object: brought *what*)
> Susana took her **sister** to the picnic. (direct object: took *whom*)
> Ren called his **mother** and **father** after the picnic. (compound direct object: called *whom*)

- Not all sentences with action verbs have a direct object. If you cannot find a word that follows an action verb and answers the question *whom* or *what*, the sentence does not have a direct object.

> Enrique came to the picnic late. (no direct object)

Animal Senses

Which underlined word in each sentence is a direct object?

1. Animals' senses help them stay alive in the wilderness.
   (A)   (B)   (C)   (D)

2. Nearly all animals can sense the difference between light and dark.
   (A)   (B)   (C) (D)

3. An animal's sense of hearing warns it that a predator may be near.
   (A) (B)   (C)   (D)

4. Touch gives information about the immediate environment.
   (A) (B)   (C)   (D)

5. A keen sense of smell helps an animal find food.
   (A) (B) (C)   (D)

6. Taste lets an animal decide if something is edible.
   (A)   (B)   (C)   (D)

7. Cats move their ears in different directions to hear a far-off sound.
   (A)   (B)   (C) (D)

8. Animals' whiskers give them information about their surroundings.
   (A) (B)   (C)   (D)

Healthful Eating Habits

9. Any doctor will tell his or her patients that maintaining good health requires a
    (A) (B)   (C)   (D)
balanced diet.

10. Milk and other dairy products introduce calcium needed for strong bones
                                      (A)   (B) (C)
and teeth.
    (D)

11. Fruits and vegetables provide fiber, which aids in digestion.
    (A)   (B)   (C)   (D)

12. Moderate amounts of meat contribute protein to the diet.
     (A)   (B)   (C)   (D)

13. Fat supplies calories to the body and is essential for proper functioning.
           (A)   (B)   (C)   (D)

14. A balanced diet of protein, carbohydrates, and fats defends the body.
    (A) (B)   (C)   (D)

15. You should minimize the amount of sweets, such as candy bars, that you eat.
                 (A)   (B)   (C) (D)

16. Garlic may cause bad breath; however, studies show that this plant has
    (A)   (B)   (C)   (D)
nutrients that might help fight certain kinds of cancer.

17. Salt adds flavor to many foods, and your body needs salt, but too much of it
        (A)   (B)   (C)   (D)
can be unhealthy.

18. A variety of cookbooks offer healthful recipes.
    (A)   (B)   (C)   (D)

19. Vegetarians eat soy for an alternative source of protein.
    (A)   (B)   (C)   (D)

20. Doctors give advice on nutrition to patients that can improve the quality of
      (A)   (B)   (C)   (D)
their lives.

Unit 13
Direct and Indirect Objects

An **indirect object** is a noun or a pronoun that answers the question *to whom, for whom, to what,* or *for what* an action is done. An indirect object appears only in a sentence that has a direct object. It appears between the action verb and the direct object. To decide if a word is an indirect object, put the word *to* or *for* before it, and change its position in the sentence.

> Monica told the **children** a story. (indirect object: *To whom* was the story told?)
> Monica told a story to the children.

> Delia made **me** a delicious breakfast. (indirect object: *For whom* was the breakfast made?)
> Delia made a delicious breakfast for me.

- A sentence may have a compound indirect object.
> Roberto gave my **sister** and **me** his place on the bus.

The Flower Sale

Identify the underlined word or words in each sentence.

21. Our school had a spring flower sale.
  (A) direct object   **(B)** indirect object

22. Our principal gave us the ground rules for the sale.
  (A) direct object   **(B)** indirect object

23. Each student received an order form.
  (A) direct object   **(B)** indirect object

24. We didn't collect any money right away.
  (A) direct object   **(B)** indirect object

25. We took orders for flowers from our families and friends.
  (A) direct object   **(B)** indirect object

26. We gave the people their flowers and collected the money then.
  (A) direct object   **(B)** indirect object

27. My family sent the hospital some flowers.
  (A) direct object   **(B)** indirect object

28. My mom secretly ordered me a bouquet of bright pink pansies.
  (A) direct object   **(B)** indirect object

29. I gave her a big hug when I saw them on the table next to my bed.
  (A) direct object   **(B)** indirect object

30. We water the flowers every morning before breakfast.
  (A) direct object   **(B)** indirect object

Nature

31. Clouds contain <u>moisture</u> that can later become rainfall.
    (A) direct object   **(B)** indirect object

32. They protect <u>us</u> from the sun's harmful rays.
    (A) direct object   **(B)** indirect object

33. Stratus clouds usually give <u>us</u> a warning that stormy weather could be on its way.
    (A) direct object   **(B)** indirect object

34. Trees give <u>people</u> shade and help to sustain life by changing carbon dioxide into oxygen, which most living things need to breathe.
    (A) direct object   **(B)** indirect object

35. Wildflowers decorate <u>fields and meadows</u> with brilliant shades of red, yellow, and orange.
    (A) compound direct object   **(B)** compound indirect object

36. A rain shower brings much-needed <u>moisture</u> to dry desert land.
    (A) direct object   **(B)** indirect object

37. A hollowed tree gives a <u>family</u> of raccoons a safe, dry place to sleep during the day.
    (A) direct object   **(B)** indirect object

38. Strong hurricane winds can severely damage <u>houses and trees</u>.
    (A) compound direct object   **(B)** compound indirect object

39. The crash and boom of the thunderstorm gave <u>my brother and me</u> a startle last night.
    (A) compound direct object   **(B)** compound indirect object

40. A tornado threatens <u>anything or anyone</u> in its path.
    (A) compound direct object   **(B)** compound indirect object

Unit 14
Appositives

An **appositive** is a noun that is placed next to another noun to identify it or add information about it. An appositive always appears next to the noun it modifies.

> Our teacher, **Ms. Hernandez**, is the Student Council advisor.

- Appositives are usually set off with commas; however, if the appositive is essential to the meaning of the sentence, commas are *not* used.

> Trish's friend **Marcus** sings in the school choir. (*essential* because Trish probably has more than one friend)

> Our principal, **Mr. Belding**, sometimes helps plan activities. (*nonessential* because there is only one principal; his name is not needed to identify him)

The Aquarium

Which underlined word in each sentence is an appositive?

1. My older sister Kareesha and I went to the aquarium last week.
   (A)   (B)   (C)   (D)

2. Our cousin Jesse told us that we had to see the new exhibit of piranha.
            (A)   (B)   (C)   (D)

3. One of my neighbors, Mrs. Fenston, studies animals, and she said that a
   (A)   (B)   (C)   (D)
   piranha is a fierce, meat-eating, freshwater fish.

4. Jake, an employee at the aquarium, told us that these fish had to be kept in a
   (A)   (B)   (C)   (D)
   separate tank.

5. He showed us a bucket containing the piranhas' food, goldfish.
                  (A)   (B)   (C)   (D)

6. I saw my friend Brenda in the crowd around the piranha tank.
                  (A)   (B)   (C)   (D)

7. Her father, Mr. Ito, said they were going to look at the eel exhibit next and
   (A)   (B)   (C) (D)
   asked if we'd like to join them.

8. We got to watch one of the eel caretakers, Chet, feed the hungry eels.
   (A)   (B)   (C)   (D)

Unit 14
Appositives

An **appositive phrase** is a group of words that includes an appositive and other words that modify the appositive. An appositive phrase is usually set off by commas and always appears next to the noun it modifies.

APPOSITIVE PHRASE

Mrs. Reynolds, **our next-door neighbor,** put her house up for sale.
(appositive phrase modifies *Mrs. Reynolds*)

Augusta, Georgia

Choose the item that is an appositive phrase and that completes each sentence.

9. Augusta, _____, was founded in 1736.
   (A) Georgia's second oldest city
   (B) bursting with beauty and charm

10. The city, _____, became an even more important center of commerce after the Civil War.
   (A) headed for a bright future
   (B) a trading center throughout the next one hundred years

11. Tourists soon made their way to Augusta, _____.
   (A) a popular winter resort today
   (B) enjoying its mild winters

12. _____, Augusta today is a vacation destination year-round.
   (A) One of my favorite cities
   (B) Hosting national golf tournaments and festivals each year

13. _____, the city has a beautiful marina area.
   (A) Located on the Savannah River
   (B) A favorite attraction of many tourists

14. Riverwalk, _____, is located in two levels along the river.
   (A) a five-block area of landscaped lawns and gardens
   (B) located in downtown Augusta

15. _____, the Augusta Golf and Gardens features life-size bronze sculptures of famous professional golfers.
   (A) Filled with a wide variety of different kinds of plants
   (B) Home of the Georgia Golf Hall of Fame

Unit 15
Gerunds

A **gerund** is a verb form that ends in *-ing* and is used as a noun. A gerund can function in the same way as other nouns. It can be a subject, a predicate noun (a noun that follows a linking verb), a direct object, or the object of a preposition.

Swimming is my favorite sport. (subject of the sentence)

My favorite sport is **swimming**. (predicate noun)

I practice **swimming** every day. (direct object)

I stay in shape by **swimming** several times a week. (object of preposition)

- Remember, a gerund must be used as a noun. Other verb forms, such as participles, also end in *-ing*. Don't confuse them with gerunds.

The **sleeping** child suddenly woke up. (participle used as an adjective describing *child*)

My dinner is **cooking** in the oven. (main verb of the verb phrase *is cooking*)

Swimming

Is the underlined word in each sentence a gerund?

1. Most people will tell you swimming is a very <u>demanding</u> sport.
   (A) Yes **(B)** No

2. <u>Practicing</u> is required twice a day by many coaches.
   (A) Yes **(B)** No

3. There are four different strokes in competitive <u>swimming</u>.
   (A) Yes **(B)** No

4. Most swimmers end up <u>specializing</u> in one or two of the strokes.
   (A) Yes **(B)** No

5. <u>Focusing</u> before a swim meet is essential.
   (A) Yes **(B)** No

6. A <u>winning</u> season requires both mental and physical training.
   (A) Yes **(B)** No

7. Working toward a goal is not always easy, but it can be <u>rewarding</u>.
   (A) Yes **(B)** No

8. Many Olympic swimmers have been <u>training</u> all their lives to compete.
   (A) Yes **(B)** No

A **gerund phrase** includes a gerund plus any other words that complete its meaning.

> **Fishing at the lake** is my dad's favorite pastime. (gerund phrase used as the subject)
>
> My favorite pastime is **playing basketball**. (gerund phrase used as a predicate noun)

- A gerund phrase must be used as a noun. Present participial phrases also have a verb form that ends in *-ing*. Don't confuse them with gerund phrases.

> **Racing down the street**, the child tripped and fell. (participial phrase describes *child*)
>
> **Racing down the street** is not a safe thing to do. (gerund phrase used as the subject)

Tennis

Is the underlined group of words in each sentence below a gerund phrase or a participial phrase?

9. Playing tennis used to be an activity for only kings and their close friends.
   (A) gerund phrase   **(B)** participial phrase

10. Beginning in the fifteenth century, this game was played only on royal indoor courts.
   (A) gerund phrase   **(B)** participial phrase

11. Late in the sixteenth century, competing on outdoor courts became common.
   (A) gerund phrase   **(B)** participial phrase

12. Tennis came to America in 1874; a visitor to England became interested in learning the game.
   (A) gerund phrase   **(B)** participial phrase

13. Bringing two tennis racquets and some tennis balls back to America, she introduced the nation to this sport.
   (A) gerund phrase   **(B)** participial phrase

14. Today, tennis is a major industry in the United States, and watching tennis is a popular spectator sport.
   (A) gerund phrase   **(B)** participial phrase

15. Training to be a professional player takes a lot of hard work and dedication.
   (A) gerund phrase   **(B)** participial phrase

A. Exercising Your Skill

You have been learning about subjects, predicates, direct and indirect objects, appositives, and gerunds. Number your paper from 1 to 4, and answer the following questions about what you have learned.

1. What is a complete subject?
   (A) all the words in the sentence
   (B) the simple subject and all the words that describe it
   (C) the simple subject only

2. Which statement is correct about the underlined words in the following sentence?
   Uncle Ray got me a bike for my birthday.
   (A) *Me* is a direct object, and *bike* is an indirect object.
   (B) *Me* is an indirect object, and *bike* is a direct object.

3. When does an appositive need commas?
   (A) when it is essential to the meaning of the sentence
   (B) when it is not essential to the meaning of the sentence
   (C) never

4. A gerund phrase acts as what in a sentence?
   (A) a noun
   (B) an adjective
   (C) an adverb

B. Expanding Your Skill

Each of the sentences below contains some words and phrases used as modifiers or nouns. Number your paper from 1 to 5. Identify each word or group of words that is underlined. Write **G** for gerund, **GP** for gerund phrase, **A** for appositive, and **AP** for appositive phrase.

1. Rosa Parks, a quiet and reserved woman, let her actions speak for her.

2. She was convicted of violating a local law.

3. Frustrated African Americans asked a respected leader, Martin Luther King Jr., to direct the bus boycott.

4. Rosa's example, an encouragement to many, sparked other nonviolent protests.

5. Protesting became common all over the South.

C. Exploring Language

Narrative Writing Read the short biography below. Number your paper from 1 to 6. Use words from the box to complete the sentences. Use the letters in parentheses within the paragraph to help you. **SS** means simple subject, **SP** means simple predicate, **DO** means direct object, **AP** means appositive phrase, and **A** means appositive.

(A) others	**(D)** gave
(B) buses	**(E)** a seamstress in Montgomery, Alabama, in 1955
(C) James	**(F)** led

Rosa Parks

Rosa Louise Parks, an African American who was born in 1913 in Tuskegee, Alabama, is a well-known figure in American history. Her father, (A) _____, was a carpenter, and her mother, Leona, was a teacher. Rosa, (AP) _____, did something that changed the course of America's future.

At that time, (SS) _____ were segregated in Alabama and throughout the South. On December 1, 1955, Rosa refused to give up her seat on a bus to a white person and was arrested. Her trial and conviction (SP) _____ to more than a year-long boycott of Montgomery buses by the African Americans of the city. The boycott resulted in a federal court decision outlawing segregation on city buses.

Rosa's courageous act inspired (DO) _____ to begin nonviolent protests against segregation all over the South. She (SP) _____ other people the courage to act through her example. The following years saw the end of segregation.

D. Expressing Yourself

Choose one of these activities. When you are finished, give your paper to your teacher.

1. Write a short biography. Perhaps you would like to write about a person in your family, school, or community. Maybe you would like to write about a person from history. You could also write about a famous person who is alive today. Remember to write in complete sentences. Use gerunds, gerund phrases, appositives, and appositive phrases to help describe the subject of the biography.

2. **WORK with a PARTNER** Pair with a partner. Decide on a topic, such as sports or music. Write five sentences about the topic you chose. Then underline the simple subject and simple predicate in each sentence. Finally, identify any other words or phrases you used. Share your labelled sentences with the class.

Unit 16
Clauses

All sentences contain at least one clause. A **clause** is a group of words that has a subject and a predicate (verb). It may be used as a sentence or as part of a sentence.

- An **independent clause,** also called a main clause, can stand alone as a sentence.

  Rachel came out of the house.

  (independent clause with subject *Rachel* and predicate *came*)

- A **dependent clause,** also called a subordinate clause, *cannot* stand alone as a sentence. It must be combined with an independent clause. Many dependent clauses begin with a subordinating conjunction, such as *after, because, since, unless,* and *when.*

  Rachel came out of the house **after we drove up**.

  (dependent clause beginning with subordinating conjunction *after*)

Songbirds

Is the group of words underlined in each sentence an independent or a dependent clause?

1. You can hear songbirds during a walk in the park.
   - **(A)** independent clause
   - **(B)** dependent clause

2. Songbirds can produce beautiful sounds because they have well-developed voice boxes.
   - **(A)** independent clause
   - **(B)** dependent clause

3. While a bird is singing, it is warning intruders to stay away from its territory.
   - **(A)** independent clause
   - **(B)** dependent clause

4. Each kind of songbird has its own special song.
   - **(A)** independent clause
   - **(B)** dependent clause

5. The mockingbird is an unusual songbird because it can add new parts to its song.
   - **(A)** independent clause
   - **(B)** dependent clause

6. When a mockingbird hears another bird's song, it copies the song and adds it to its own song.
   - **(A)** independent clause
   - **(B)** dependent clause

7. Although you may not believe it, crows are considered to be songbirds.
   - **(A)** independent clause
   - **(B)** dependent clause

8. The chickadee gets its name from the sound it makes when it sings.
   - **(A)** independent clause
   - **(B)** dependent clause

Unit 16
Clauses

- A dependent clause can come before or after an independent clause in a sentence. When the dependent clause comes before the independent clause, the two clauses are separated by a comma.

  When the storm was over, we started for home.

- When the dependent clause follows the independent clause and acts as an adverb, there is usually no comma separating the two clauses.

  We hurried home **because it was getting dark**.

New Haven, Connecticut

Is the group of words underlined in each sentence an independent or dependent clause?

9. <u>When the Puritans founded New Haven in 1638</u>, they planned the city in a series of nine squares, with one larger square in the middle.
   (A) independent clause   **(B)** dependent clause

10. Today that central square remains as <u>those early settlers plotted it</u>.
    (A) independent clause   **(B)** dependent clause

11. <u>The square is called the Green</u> because it is sixteen acres of grass with only three buildings on it.
    (A) independent clause   **(B)** dependent clause

12. <u>The Green belongs to the people of New Haven</u>.
    (A) independent clause   **(B)** dependent clause

13. <u>Although the Green is very beautiful</u>, it is not the only attraction in New Haven to see.
    (A) independent clause   **(B)** dependent clause

14. <u>If you visit New Haven</u>, don't miss seeing Yale University, one of the oldest universities in America.
    (A) independent clause   **(B)** dependent clause

15. Yale was founded in 1701 <u>after New Haven had been in existence for sixty-three years</u>.
    (A) independent clause   **(B)** dependent clause

16. <u>Before Yale moved to New Haven in 1716</u>, it was known as the Collegiate School.
    (A) independent clause   **(B)** dependent clause

Unit 16
Clauses

An **adverb clause** is a dependent, or subordinate, clause that often modifies the verb in the independent, or main, clause of the sentence. An adverb clause tells *when, where, how, why, to what degree,* or *under what conditions* the action of the verb takes place.

> **After we picked the apples,** we made applesauce. (clause tells *when* and modifies *made*)

- Adverb clauses can also modify state-of-being verbs.

> It will be delicious **because we used a great recipe**. (clause tells *why* and modifies *be*)

- A subordinating conjunction introduces an adverb clause.

> I can't wait **until we can eat it**! (*until* is a subordinating conjunction)

Common Subordinating Conjunctions

after	because	since	till	when
although	before	than	unless	whenever
as	if	though	until	where

Lacrosse

Is the underlined group of words an adverb clause?

17. Before the first Europeans arrived in the New World, Native Americans were playing the game of lacrosse.
    (A) Yes   **(B)** No

18. As Native Americans originally played it, the game might have a thousand players on each side with goals miles apart.
    (A) Yes   **(B)** No

19. A game of lacrosse regularly lasted for three days.
    (A) Yes   **(B)** No

20. Each player was supposed to disable as many opponents as he could.
    (A) Yes   **(B)** No

21. Only then would the player be able to concentrate on making a goal.
    (A) Yes   **(B)** No

22. Though it is certainly a rough sport, modern lacrosse is not as dangerous as it used to be.
    (A) Yes   **(B)** No

Corn

23. Corn is the only grain that is native to America.
    (A) Yes   **(B)** No

24. Before Columbus or any other European arrived, corn was being grown.
    (A) Yes   **(B)** No

25. It was first grown in South America as long ago as 3000 B.C.
    (A) Yes   **(B)** No

26. Native Americans developed corn by cross-breeding a variety of grasses.
    (A) Yes   **(B)** No

27. Called *maize* by the Native Americans, corn was a valuable crop because it was resistant to disease.
    (A) Yes   **(B)** No

28. Eventually corn spread to Europe; Columbus took seeds back to Spain after he completed his second trip to America in 1496.
    (A) Yes   **(B)** No

29. In addition to its delicious taste, corn has many uses.
    (A) Yes   **(B)** No

30. Ethanol from corn powers cars and a variety of other engines.
    (A) Yes   **(B)** No

31. Corn syrup can replace imported sugar as a sweetener in candy and soda.
    (A) Yes   **(B)** No

32. Feed for cattle, hogs, and poultry is the largest market for corn.
    (A) Yes   **(B)** No

33. Where soil is fertile, a single acre of land can produce more than seven million kernels of corn.
    (A) Yes   **(B)** No

34. Each kernel of corn has the potential to grow an ear containing 800 kernels.
    (A) Yes   **(B)** No

Unit 16
Clauses

An **adjective clause** is a type of dependent clause that modifies a noun or a pronoun in the main clause of a sentence and answers the questions *what kind, how many,* or *which one* or *ones.* An adjective clause is usually introduced by a **relative pronoun.** The relative pronouns are *that, which, who, whom,* and *whose.*

> The movie **that we saw last night** was very exciting. (clause modifies *movie*)

- Often a relative pronoun that begins an adjective clause acts as the subject of the clause.
> My sister, **who usually doesn't care for action films**, really liked it. (*who* is the subject of the adjective clause that modifies *sister*)

- An adjective clause can also begin with *where* or *when.*
> I remember a time **when she left in the middle of a movie.** (clause modifies *time*)

Braille

Is the group of words underlined in each sentence an adjective clause or an adverb clause?

35. Braille, <u>which is a system of reading and writing for the blind</u>, is based on a code of sixty-three characters.
    (A) adjective clause   **(B)** adverb clause

36. This system was invented by sixteen-year-old Louis Braille, <u>who had been blind since the age of three</u>.
    (A) adjective clause   **(B)** adverb clause

37. Louis attended a school for the blind; he was concerned about the school library <u>because it had only fourteen books with raised letters</u>.
    (A) adjective clause   **(B)** adverb clause

38. The blind students <u>who tried to use these books</u> soon gave up reading in frustration.
    (A) adjective clause   **(B)** adverb clause

39. Louis began experimenting and eventually had a system <u>that would work</u>.
    (A) adjective clause   **(B)** adverb clause

40. <u>After the other students at the school learned about the system</u>, they were enthusiastic about it and used it regularly.
    (A) adjective clause   **(B)** adverb clause

Unit 16
Clauses

State Names

41. Toponymy, <u>which is the study of the origins of place names</u>, provides some interesting information about the names of states.
(A) adjective clause   **(B)** adverb clause

42. <u>While the names of all states have some kind of origin</u>, many of them come from Native American words.
(A) adjective clause   **(B)** adverb clause

43. Iowa, <u>which means "the sleepy ones,"</u> and Michigan, which means "big water," are examples.
(A) adjective clause   **(B)** adverb clause

44. The name Mississippi comes from an Indian word <u>that means "father of waters."</u>
(A) adjective clause   **(B)** adverb clause

45. Other states come from the names of European kings and queens <u>because the states had originally been established as colonies by the monarchs.</u>
(A) adjective clause   **(B)** adverb clause

46. Some examples <u>that come to mind</u> are Louisiana from King Louis of France, Georgia from King George of England, and Maryland from Queen Mary of England.
(A) adjective clause   **(B)** adverb clause

47. California's name comes from the Spanish word *Califerne,* <u>which is the name of an imaginary land in a Spanish sixteenth-century novel.</u>
(A) adjective clause   **(B)** adverb clause

48. <u>Even though we know the origins of most states' names</u>, some are still a mystery.
(A) adjective clause   **(B)** adverb clause

49. <u>Although it is believed to be an Indian name</u>, Idaho has an uncertain word origin.
(A) adjective clause   **(B)** adverb clause

50. The state of Washington was named after George Washington, <u>who was our nation's first president</u>.
(A) adjective clause   **(B)** adverb clause

Types of Sentences

- A **simple sentence** has one complete subject and one complete predicate. The subject, predicate, or both may be compound.

> The **rain had fallen** steadily for days. (simple subject and simple predicate)
>
> The **rain** and **wind caused** much damage. (compound subject and simple predicate)
>
> The **rain pounded** and **lashed** at the boats in the harbor. (simple subject and compound predicate)

- A **compound sentence** contains two or more simple sentences, which are called independent, or main, clauses. Independent clauses in a compound sentence are connected by a comma plus a conjunction or by a semicolon.

> The rain poured**, and** the waters in the river kept rising.
>
> The townspeople made a decision**;** they stacked sandbags along the river's banks.

Comic Strips

Is each sentence below a simple sentence or a compound sentence?

1. Comic strips began to appear in the United States during the late nineteenth century.
   (A) simple sentence   **(B)** compound sentence

2. By 1915, black-and-white comic strips were regularly appearing in daily newspapers; they were immensely popular with readers.
   (A) simple sentence   **(B)** compound sentence

3. "Winnie Winkle" was created in 1920; it was the first career-woman comic strip.
   (A) simple sentence   **(B)** compound sentence

4. "Blondie" was created in 1930, and it soon achieved fame all over the world.
   (A) simple sentence   **(B)** compound sentence

5. "Flash Gordon" became the first space-age comic strip.
   (A) simple sentence   **(B)** compound sentence

6. In 1937, "Superman" came on the scene as the first superhero with superpowers.
   (A) simple sentence   **(B)** compound sentence

Unit 17
Types of Sentences

A **complex sentence** has one independent clause and one or more dependent clauses. A dependent clause may function as an adjective clause or an adverb clause.

> The trees **that have pink and white blossoms** are beautiful. (adjective clause)

> We will enjoy the flowering trees **while we can**. (adverb clause)

Circuses

Is each sentence below a simple, a compound, or a complex sentence?

7. The first circus dates back to Rome in the first century B.C.
(A) simple sentence   (B) compound sentence   (C) complex sentence

8. The modern traveling circus began in England in 1768; it quickly spread to France.
(A) simple sentence   (B) compound sentence   (C) complex sentence

9. Phillip Astley, who first developed the idea of the modern circus, started with trick riding stunts.
(A) simple sentence   (B) compound sentence   (C) complex sentence

10. Soon he added other types of performances, which provided more variety.
(A) simple sentence   (B) compound sentence   (C) complex sentence

11. The crowds were delighted by the jugglers, aerial acrobats, tightrope walkers, and gymnasts.
(A) simple sentence   (B) compound sentence   (C) complex sentence

12. Today, circuses that provide thrills and chills to their audiences perform all over the world.
(A) simple sentence   (B) compound sentence   (C) complex sentence

13. When P. T. Barnum and James Bailey joined forces in 1887, history was made.
(A) simple sentence   (B) compound sentence   (C) complex sentence

14. Barnum and Bailey's Circus is one of the most popular American circuses in existence today.
(A) simple sentence   (B) compound sentence   (C) complex sentence

A **compound-complex** sentence contains two or more independent clauses and one or more dependent clauses.

INDEPENDENT CLAUSE   DEPENDENT CLAUSE

The firefighters stayed on the scene **until all the injured were taken to a hospital,** and the police officers assisted.

DEPENDENT CLAUSE   INDEPENDENT CLAUSE
(continued)

Balloons

Is each sentence below a compound-complex sentence?

15. The idea of flying a hot-air balloon originated in France in 1783.
   (A) Yes   **(B)** No, it is a simple sentence.

16. Almost immediately, the hydrogen-filled balloon came on the scene.
   (A) Yes   **(B)** No, it is a simple sentence.

17. Hydrogen was an improvement over hot air because hydrogen is lighter than air.
   (A) Yes   **(B)** No, it is a complex sentence.

18. The first of these balloons, though it was made of varnished silk and measured over fifteen feet, made a trip of fifteen miles from the launch site; it came to rest near a small farming village.
   (A) Yes   **(B)** No, it is a complex sentence.

19. The farmers, who had never seen anything like this balloon before, were frightened by this object descending through the clouds.
   (A) Yes   **(B)** No, it is a complex sentence.

20. They attacked the "monster," which the farmers feared greatly, with pitchforks and scythes; before long, they had completely destroyed the balloon.
   (A) Yes   **(B)** No, it is a compound sentence.

21. Whereas early hot-air balloons were heavier by today's standards, modern hot-air balloons are constructed of lighter man-made materials, and they are powered by burning propane stored in tanks.
   (A) Yes   **(B)** No, it is a complex sentence.

22. There are even balloon races, which officials measure for accuracy of flying rather than for speed; hot-air balloons are propelled by wind and cannot be manually sped up or slowed down.
   (A) Yes   **(B)** No, it is a compound sentence.

Calendar Facts

Which kind of sentence is each sentence below?

23. The names of the days of the week come from two sources.
    (A) simple   **(C)** complex
    (B) compound   **(D)** compound-complex

24. Tuesday, Wednesday, Thursday, and Friday got their names from Norse mythological characters; this family of four, who were named Tiu, Woden, Thor, and Frigg, had different names in different countries, but they were the same characters.
    (A) simple   **(C)** complex
    (B) compound   **(D)** compound-complex

25. Tiu, who was also known as Tyr, was the Norse god of war.
    (A) simple   **(C)** complex
    (B) compound   **(D)** compound-complex

26. Woden, or Odin, was the Norse god of victory.
    (A) simple   **(C)** complex
    (B) compound   **(D)** compound-complex

27. Thor was the Norse god of thunder; he was the oldest son of Woden.
    (A) simple   **(C)** complex
    (B) compound   **(D)** compound-complex

28. Frigg, who was the mother of Tiu and Thor, was the wife of Woden; she was the goddess of love.
    (A) simple   **(C)** complex
    (B) compound   **(D)** compound-complex

29. There are many similarities among names of the days of the week across different languages.
    (A) simple   **(C)** complex
    (B) compound   **(D)** compound-complex

30. There are 365 days in one calendar year, but every so many years there are 366 days.
    (A) simple   **(C)** complex
    (B) compound   **(D)** compound-complex

Vincent van Gogh

Which kind of sentence is each sentence below?

31. Vincent van Gogh is probably one of the greatest painters of all time.
    - **(A)** simple
    - **(B)** compound
    - **(C)** complex
    - **(D)** compound-complex

32. The vitality that he uses in his paintings is amazing, and his colors are so vibrant.
    - **(A)** simple
    - **(B)** compound
    - **(C)** complex
    - **(D)** compound-complex

33. It is hard to believe, but his work was rejected by most people while he was still alive.
    - **(A)** simple
    - **(B)** compound
    - **(C)** complex
    - **(D)** compound-complex

34. They were disturbed by the bright colors and bold, swirling brushstrokes; nobody wanted his paintings.
    - **(A)** simple
    - **(B)** compound
    - **(C)** complex
    - **(D)** compound-complex

35. After van Gogh's death, the world began to appreciate his genius, and now his paintings are considered to be valuable masterpieces.
    - **(A)** simple
    - **(B)** compound
    - **(C)** complex
    - **(D)** compound-complex

36. Today his paintings are treasured by the museums that own them.
    - **(A)** simple
    - **(B)** compound
    - **(C)** complex
    - **(D)** compound-complex

37. The information that we have about van Gogh's life comes mainly from letters that he wrote to his brother Theo.
    - **(A)** simple
    - **(B)** compound
    - **(C)** complex
    - **(D)** compound-complex

38. The two brothers once lived together in Paris, which is where van Gogh learned some of his painting techniques.
    - **(A)** simple
    - **(B)** compound
    - **(C)** complex
    - **(D)** compound-complex

39. The painting "Starry Night" is perhaps one of his most famous works of art.
    - **(A)** simple
    - **(B)** compound
    - **(C)** complex
    - **(D)** compound-complex

Unit 17
Types of Sentences

I. M. Pei

40. I. M. Pei is an architect who has the ability to see things in a new way.
- **(A)** simple
- **(B)** compound
- **(C)** complex
- **(D)** compound-complex

41. Since he started working after graduating in 1946, people all over the world have admired his building designs.
- **(A)** simple
- **(B)** compound
- **(C)** complex
- **(D)** compound-complex

42. Pei is interested in the space around the building that he designs, and he uses that space to great effect.
- **(A)** simple
- **(B)** compound
- **(C)** complex
- **(D)** compound-complex

43. His designs place a building in its setting like a jewel in a ring.
- **(A)** simple
- **(B)** compound
- **(C)** complex
- **(D)** compound-complex

44. He relies on abstract form to plan his buildings, but he uses concrete materials such as stone, glass, and steel to complete them.
- **(A)** simple
- **(B)** compound
- **(C)** complex
- **(D)** compound-complex

45. I. M. Pei's buildings are known by their beauty and their compatibility with their environment.
- **(A)** simple
- **(B)** compound
- **(C)** complex
- **(D)** compound-complex

46. He has designed nearly fifty projects, and over half of them have won major awards.
- **(A)** simple
- **(B)** compound
- **(C)** complex
- **(D)** compound-complex

47. The Rock and Roll Hall of Fame in Cleveland, Ohio, was designed by Pei.
- **(A)** simple
- **(B)** compound
- **(C)** complex
- **(D)** compound-complex

48. His design of a world-famous museum in Paris was controversial because people did not understand the design at first, but they later came to respect it.
- **(A)** simple
- **(B)** compound
- **(C)** complex
- **(D)** compound-complex

A. Exercising Your Skill

You have been learning about different kinds of clauses and types of sentences. Number your paper from 1 to 4, and answer the following questions about what you have learned.

1. What kind of clause modifies a noun or a pronoun?
   (A) an adverb clause
   (B) an adjective clause
   (C) an independent clause

2. What kind of clause can always stand alone?
   (A) an adjective clause
   (B) a dependent clause
   (C) an independent clause

3. Identify the clause in this sentence.
   The tool that you are looking for is in the garage.
   (A) adverb clause
   (B) adjective clause

4. Which type of sentence includes two or more independent clauses and one or more dependent clauses?
   (A) a compound-complex sentence
   (B) a compound sentence
   (C) a complex sentence

B. Expanding Your Skill

Number your paper from 1 to 5. Read and identify each group of words. Write **S** if the group of words is a simple sentence. Write **CP** if the group of words is a compound sentence. Write **CX** if the group of words is a complex sentence. Write **CPCX** if the group of words is a compound-complex sentence.

1. *The Hobbit* was written by J. R. R. Tolkien.

2. The main character is Bilbo, who is a hobbit.

3. The book is the story of Bilbo's great adventure.

4. He and his friends succeed in their quest, and after many adventures, Bilbo returns home.

5. At the end of the story, the ring is safe in Bilbo's house, but even though the story ends, we know that we haven't heard the last of that ring.

C. Exploring Language

Expository Writing Read the book review below. Number your paper from 1 to 8. Identify each underlined group of words. Write **I** if the group of words is an independent clause. Write **D** if the group of words is a dependent clause.

Island of the Blue Dolphins

(1) The author of this book is Scott O'Dell. It is the story of a twelve-year-old girl's life alone on an island in the Pacific Ocean. She was mistakenly left behind **(2)** when her people sailed away, never to return. **(3)** The girl's name was Karana, and she wanted nothing more than to see a ship on the horizon **(4)** that would take her away. But she had to wait a long time, and **(5)** her life wasn't easy. She had to provide herself with food and shelter. She also had to make weapons to protect herself from the wild dogs that lived on the island. **(6)** This book was very good **(7)** because it had many exciting events. It also made me think about how I would have acted **(8)** if I had been in Karana's situation.

D. Expressing Yourself

Choose one of these activities. When you are finished, give your paper to your teacher.

1. **WORK with a PARTNER** Write a book review of a book that you have read. Be sure to include the author's name in your review. Write four or five sentences that tell what the book is about. End your review by explaining what you liked about the book. Exchange papers with a partner. Look at each sentence in your partner's book review. How many simple, compound, and complex sentences are there? Can you find a compound-complex sentence?

2. On a sheet of paper, write the name of the author of your favorite book. Find information about him or her on the Internet or in another book, and write a short four-sentence biography about him or her. Find and circle any independent clauses, and underline the dependent clauses in your biography. Put a box around any adverb clauses or adjective clauses. Inside the box, write **ADV** for an adverb clause or **ADJ** for an adjective clause.

GRAMMAR Scope and Sequence • Specific Skill Series for Language Arts

Unit/Level	Level A	Level B	Level C	Level D	Level E	Level F	Level G	Level H
Unit 1	Nouns	Nouns	Nouns	Nouns	Nouns	Nouns	Nouns	Nouns
Unit 2	Singular and Plural Nouns	Singular and Plural Nouns	Singular and Plural Nouns	Possessive Nouns	Possessive Nouns	Possessive Nouns	Possessive Nouns	Possessive Nouns
Unit 3	Possessive Nouns	Possessive Nouns	Possessive Nouns	Subject and Object Pronouns	Subject and Object Pronouns	Subject and Object Pronouns	Subject and Object Pronouns	Subject and Object Pronouns
Unit 4	Pronouns	Pronouns	Pronouns	Possessive Pronouns	Possessive Pronouns	Possessive Pronouns	Possessive Pronouns	Possessive Pronouns
Unit 5	Possessive Pronouns	Possessive Pronouns	Subject and Object Pronouns	Pronouns	Pronouns	Pronouns	Pronouns	Pronouns
Unit 6	Verbs	Interrogative Pronouns	Possessive Pronouns	Pronouns	Pronouns	Pronouns	Pronouns	Pronouns
Unit 7	Helping Verbs	Verbs	Interrogative Pronouns	Verbs	Verbs	Verbs	Verbs	Verbs
Unit 8	Adjectives	Helping Verbs	Verbs	Adjectives	Adjectives	Adjectives	Adjectives	Adjectives
Unit 9	Parts of a Sentence	Adjectives	Adjectives	Adverbs	Adverbs	Adverbs	Adverbs	Adverbs
Unit 10	Parts of a Sentence	Adverbs	Adverbs	Prepositions	Prepositions	Prepositions	Prepositions	Prepositions
Unit 11	Changing Sentences into Questions	Prepositions	Prepositions	Interjections and Conjunctions	Conjunctions	Conjunctions	Conjunctions	Conjunctions
Unit 12	Changing Sentences into Questions	Conjunctions	Prepositions	Subjects and Predicates	Subjects and Predicates	Subjects and Predicates	Subjects and Predicates	Subjects and Predicates
Unit 13		Interjections	Conjunctions	Direct Objects	Direct and Indirect Objects	Direct and Indirect Objects	Direct and Indirect Objects	Direct and Indirect Objects
Unit 14		Parts of a Sentence	Interjections	Clauses	Appositives	Appositives	Appositives	Appositives
Unit 15		Compound Subjects and Predicates	Subjects and Predicates	Clauses	Clauses	Gerunds	Gerunds	Gerunds
Unit 16		Changing Sentences into Questions	Compound Subjects and Predicates	Types of Sentences	Types of Sentences	Infinitives	Infinitives	Infinitives
Unit 17		Changing Sentences into Questions	Complete Subjects and Predicates			Clauses	Clauses	Clauses
Unit 18			Types of Sentences			Types of Sentences	Types of Sentences	Clauses
Unit 19			Changing Sentences into Questions					Types of Sentences